Connected Islands

Poetry by Naomi Long Madgett:

Songs to a Phantom Nightingale
One and the Many
Star by Star
Pink Ladies in the Afternoon
Phantom Nightingale: Juvenilia
Exits and Entrances
Octavia and Other Poems
Octavia: Guthrie and Beyond
Remembrances of Spring: Collected Early Poems
Connected Islands: New and Selected Poems

Connected Islands

New and Selected Poems

by

Naomi Long Madgett

Naomi Long Madgett

Lotus Press
Detroit

First Edition

International Standard Book Number 0-916418-94-4

Printed in the United States of America

Lotus Press, Inc.
"Flower of a New Nile"
Post Office Box 21607
Detroit, Michigan 48221

www.lotuspress.org

Acknowledgments

Grateful acknowledgment is made to the following publications in which some of these poems first appeared: *The Virginia Statesman, Freedomways, Phylon, Callaloo, The Black Scholar, Negro Digest, Black World, African American Review, Green River Review, Poet, Drumvoices Revue, Michigan Quarterly Review, Obsidian, Images from the African Diaspora* (in collaboration with artist Carl Owens), and *Adam of Ifé: Black Women in Praise of Black Men.*

The author also wishes to thank Terry Blackhawk, Jill Witherspoon Boyer, Paulette Childress, Leisia Duskin, and Monifa A. Love for their helpful suggestions.

The following poems are included in earlier collections as indicated: "Reply" from *One and the Many;* "Alabama Centennial," "Midway," "Mortality," "Refuge," "Tree of Heaven," and "Trinity: A Dream Sequence, #18" from *Star by Star;* "Grand Circus Park," "Nocturne II: Still," "Souvenir," and "Sylvester Expelled" from *Pink Ladies in the Afternoon;* "City Nights," "Fifth Street Exit, Richmond," "The Old Women," "Packrat," and "Phillis" from *Exits and Entrances;* and "Jogging at the Health Club," "At Midday," "The Last Happy Day," "Letting It All Hang Out," "Memorial," "On Corcovado Mountain," "Remember Bahia," "Soon I Will Be Done," "'The Sun Do Move,'" "Twice a Child," and "Without Condition" from *Octavia and Other Poems.* "Even Me," "Make Thy Way Plain," "Pilot Me," "Great Is Thy Faithfulness," "Stand by Me," "To Have a Home," and "At the River I Stand" first appeared as a limited edition of a set of signed and numbered broadsides under the title, *Hymns Are My Prayers.*

For Jill and Malaika

Connected Islands

Contents

Connected Islands   *1*

I.

Genesis: The Missing Chapter   5
That Universal Something   7
Abandoned   8
Fragments of a Dream   9
Jogging at the Health Club   10
Grand Circus Park   11
Boy on a Bicycle   12
Fifth Street Exit, Richmond   13
On Corcovado Mountain   17
Remember Bahia   18
Seagulls in the City   20
First Man   21
Sisters of the Sun   22

II.

Soon I Will Be Done   25
The Old Women   27
Phillis   28
"The Sun Do Move"   31
The Master Calls   33
Tree of Heaven   36
Alabama Centennial   37
Midway   39
Even Me   40
Make Thy Way Plain   42

Pilot Me   43

Great Is Thy Faithfulness   45

Stand by Me   47

To Have a Home   49

At the River I Stand   51

III.

Attitude at 75   55

Letting It All Hang Out   56

Glories of the Morning   58

My Mother's Roses   59

Beach Scene   60

At Midday   62

Twice a Child   63

Reluctant Light   64

Memorial   66

Lonely Eagle   67

He Lives in Me   68

Reply   70

IV.

Souvenir   73

Nocturne II: Still   74

Trinity: A Dream Sequence #18   75

Severance   76

Without Condition   77

Packrat   79

Sylvester Expelled   80

Images   81

And When   82

A Thousand Goodbyes   83

The Last Happy Day 85
Refuge 89
Mortality 90
City Nights 91
Renewal 93

About the Author *95*

Connected Islands

Disjointed words and phrases come to me
in dreams like scattered islands. Rising

from secret places, they flow to the surface
of consciousness, spill onto empty pages.

But I tell you this: They will all come together.
Everything means and nothing is isolated.

Rock-a-bye baby on the tree top . . .
A mother in Africa rocks her infant

dying of starvation, belly distended.
When the bough breaks . . . A sergeant,

in Baltimore on furlough, scribbles a note
before she leaps from a ninth floor ledge.

"So long, Badness. I did love you. See you there."
Her broken bones lie at awkward angles on the sidewalk.

The next week, her married soldier lover follows her
in suicide. *I cover the waterfront* searching for *a love*

that cannot live yet never dies. A woman shivers
under the boardwalk in Atlantic City with only a box

for shelter. In a funeral home in London
the ringlet-covered head of a year-old baby

rests on a pillow in a small white casket. Nearby
the shriveled hands of a woman in her nineties

hold a rose. *With His sheep securely fold you.*
The space between them is heavy with formaldehyde,

ends and beginnings. *Change and decay . . . .*
They are alone, they are together.

Even separate islands are connected by some sea
and we are sisters touching across the waters

of our disparate lives, singing our untold stories
in a harmony of undulating waves.

I.

Genesis: The Missing Chapter

And when God had created the world and all things in it
and sat down on the seventh day to rest from his labors,
he was pleased with his view of mountains
and islands of clouds floating in a sea-blue sky.
He delighted in the scent of hyacinths and frankincense
and the taste of salt and honey.
The bark of trees and the fur of rabbits
were pleasant to his touch.

But when humans uttered sound,
their speech fell like a dull thud, earthbound —
a babble, discordant to his ear. And he said,
"There is something I have forgotten, something
I still must do." And he thought and thought about it
until he noticed the trilling of a tiny bird.

So on the eighth day, God took the lilt of birds
and called it Joy.
He borrowed the rhythm of the ocean
and called it Supplication.
The roar of thunder he named Despair.
He gathered the many voices of the wind
and called them Exaltation,
and he named the rustle of leaves Thanksgiving.

The whisper of rain became Love
and the murmur of a brook, Faith and Hope.

He bound them all together and called them Music
and planted it in the human voice.

Then he created poets
so that music could be sung in words.

And choirs rejoiced, organs consecrated,
violins implored, drums celebrated,
clarinets wailed, trumpets praised,
trombones lamented,
and saxophones glorified God in the highest.

And God said, "Now my world is truly complete.
Hereafter, whenever humans seek to communicate
with each other and with me,
music will forever be the purest vehicle
for carrying the varied messages of the soul."

That Universal Something

(for James Earl Jones)

There is a universal something
that makes us want to sing.

It takes exterminators to flush out
some creatures from the dark

but no Pied Piper is required to lure the poets
from their secret places and lead them to the light.

It isn't Art they follow, it's both the need
for water to quench an ancient thirst and

a bubbling over like lava when a volcano
erupts and has to spill out somewhere.

Writing a poem is that universal something
we sometimes have to do.

Abandoned

my muse has left me has crept from my bed in the night
she has stolen my images flown to the treetops
to give them to sparrows for straw in their nests
has fled to the seashore and buried my metaphors in sand
where waves will lap them up she has scattered my song
to the wind has left me without a note of goodbye
on the nightstand a kiss a caress she has
stripped me of spirit and soul Euterpe has left me
alone and tuneless and naked and cold and I
am nothing without her

Fragments of a Dream

A letter has fallen out of my name. It tumbles
over and over itself. I can't retrieve it
and without it I don't know who I am.

I follow it to St. Mark's Square but it turns
into pigeons that turn into worms. Everywhere
I step they squish and squirm and I have no wings.

I am clinging to the edge of a star trying to capture
the missing letter. I can't hold on much longer.
I will disintegrate before I hit the earth.

Even the smallest deletion changes the alphabet,
the order of the universe, as a stuck piano key
alters a song, and I am falling, incomplete, anonymous.

My heart still pulsing, I feel the air move as the lid
of my coffin is lowered. My mouth is full of sand
and I can't cry out for someone to give me back my self.

I want to die easy when I die. This is no way
to go, sod heavy on my chest. My eyes are glued shut
and I can't read the name on my headstone.

Jogging at the Health Club

In mirrors reflected in mirrors
I meet myself coming and going
I leave by the same doors I enter
the rooms I inhabit instantly vanish

Through doubled eyes I watch my face dividing
colliding with itself: splintered
selves casting many-colored prisms
in all directions at once folding
into themselves reappearing
devouring, multiplying

On such a runway do I recognize
refractions of my self accepting
that all things are divisible that
one's sum of parts is other
than a whole

Grand Circus Park
(Twenty Years Later)

Old men still drowse on gray park benches
watching a dubious sun leak through
the dying branches of elms.
> "The axe shall be laid (Hew, hew!)
> to the root of the trees . . . "

It is hard to realize
they are not the same old men,
grizzled and bleary-eyed as memories.

Bold, raucous pigeons flaunt themselves
before the glazed, glaucomic stares.
Young mothers quickly look away, caress
with special tenderness their infants' proper curls.
> " . . . and every tree that bringeth not forth
> good fruit . . . "

The Cadillac bus still stops at the same spot,
but the passengers are not the same
and the point of exit is no longer home.
Even the wind is dying, and an autumn fog
settles like a shroud upon the old men's shoulders.
Do they dream of sputtering logs
in open fireplaces,
or do they shake with the impotent rage of trees
> "hewn down and cast into the fire"?

Boy on a Bicycle

(Summer Solstice, Detroit)

Slim bluejeaned legs pump laboriously
up a wet incline while a steady drizzle
films a dark young face with satin mist.
Summer vacation has just begun.

It is midmorning, the twenty-first of June.
The daylight will be longer than any other
day of an uncertain year, but it is doubtful
that anyone will see the sun. The streets
are slick and treacherous.

Where is he going, young black boy
in a city full of clouds and shadows,
pedaling two wheels up a hill in the rain?

Fifth Street Exit, Richmond

1.

Leave the freeway at this point.
Drive off where a chainlink fence
separates the road from a patch of weeds
and forces you past a row of ancient houses dying
from the fever of progress. Hurry past.
Proceed with cautious speed down Fifth Street
to Main, beyond the place where death lurks, where
airy ghosts peer through the dust of floor-long
windows and scream with hollow voiceless mouths.

2.

The phantom children are calling,
they are calling my name.
They are playing hide-and-seek
by yellow streetlight and
they cannot find me. I am busy
chasing fireflies.
The phantom children are calling,
calling my name.

3.

I could go back if I wanted to.
I could join the dance again
bouncing my feet with theirs
on the sidewalk of uneven brick
as they jump   jump

13

and jump   Jim   Crow.
I could learn again to make
the swooping gesture
        Cotton needs a-pickin' so-o-o bad
in rhythm with their song
(graceless newcomer from the North
but eager to be one with them).
        Cotton needs a-pickin' so-o-o bad
        I'm gonna pick all over this land.
I *could* do it again.
If I wanted to.

4.

The clop-clop-clop of horses' hooves,
the clatter of wagon wheels on cobblestones
bring the street vendor to the shade
of our magnolias.

Above the horses' whinnying
his cindery voice, half-song, half-wail,
bellows, blasts across
the heavy air.

        Get your fresh watermelon,
        Sweet melon, cold melon,
        Black-seeded juicy melon,
        Ripe melon sweet.

14

Oh, the spicy redolence of summer!
Oh, the freshfruit glories of Southern
summertime!

> *Watermelon, sweet melon,*
> *Black-seeded fresh melon,*
> *Come buy your watermelon,*
> *Ripe melon sweet.*

5.

Wil and Clarence and Dadie and Lew
played mumble-de-peg by the curb, and Suzie
whimpered and put up her hair in balls
while Bubba chased me around the yard, and

Grampa died and Bubba cried
and knocked me down and gashed my head
and Dadie's father stitched my wound
and Sadie cut my hair that summer

and seasons came and long years went
and Richmond just kept coming back
and we were grown before we guessed
the wonder that those summers meant.

6.

I wish I *could* go back
to the cool green shuttered dark
that hid us from the boisterous sun,

from the explosion of color and fragrance outside,
back into the cocoon,
back to the Concord grapes ripening
in the arbor where the swing hung still
patient   waiting   for the evening cool —
afternoon baths and starched white
eyelet dresses with blue sashes
and patent leather shoes:

> Richmond summers chocolate
> as childhood's toothsomest delights.

I wish I could.

7.

Azalea petals fell for the last time
one spring and tried in vain
to fertilize this asphalt garden.
The bricks crumbled and were hauled away,
the green shutters fell to dust
and where Grandma's white-pillared porch
once welcomed Sunday callers
a chainlink fence went up to mark an exit
from Wherever, U.S.A. to Main Street, Richmond.

Leave the freeway at this point and don't,
oh, don't go back. Don't listen
to the children's hollow voices
chanting elegies to the whir
of wheels turning, turning.

On Corcovado Mountain

High above the sands
of Rio, clouds veil
the impassive face

of the Redeemer.
Momentarily
pale sunlight steals through

seeking refuge in
folds of the stiffly
fluted skirt. Below

in deeper shadows,
in crevices of
precarious hills

crouch faceless squalid
children whom those out
stretched arms will never
hold, never redeem.

Remember Bahia

(Lembrança do Senhor do Bonfim da Bahia)

Stumbling into someone else's dream,
came to old Pelhourinho.
Climbed the steep cobblestones
where African women hawked their sweet
concoctions in Portuguese.
Entered through narrow doorways
to watch ballooning white skirts swirl
around black ankles dancing in praise
of Yoruba deities. And in Felinto's art shop,
soothed the carved nail-torn hands of a writhing Christ.
(Beneath scarred ebony feet
entwined in agony, mask of an African
endures with dry impassive eyes.)

At the Church of the Good End,
hung up my home-lost spirit
among the wounded plastic limbs
of those who came to pray for miracles
and left it there.

Stumbled into someone else's dream
and made it mine.

Seagulls in the City

Seagulls fly inland from the Detroit River
to scrounge in the debris of supermarket parking lots.

Their black-tipped wings circle with elegance and grace,
rise, and then descend to perch on light posts.

Shoppers returning to their cars with bags of groceries
curse the excrement dropped on their windshields.

But the gulls' airy cries connect me to all waters I have
                    known.
Our mothers must have heard them on the Nile

and shackled to the walls on Gorée Island
before they lost the sungold shores of home.

Slaves in Bahia and the cotton fields along the Mississippi
listened as they flung their discontent into the wind.

And we, like seagulls, settle on posts of light,
seeking sustenance in history's discarded pages.

First Man

(for Carl Owens, in memoriam)

Sculpted from the clay of Africa,
first man in all the universe,
you were created in the image of a tree.
Transplanted now to foreign soil,
you are still wondrous in your towering vigor
and amplitude, and in the shade you give.

Tender birch or seasoned oak, mahogany or cedar,
baobab or ebony, you are the joy of a new Eden,
crested with leaves as varied
as fades and dreadlocks.

Your countenance, like rings of a stalwart trunk,
tells the unmatched story
of how you persevered and flourished
in spite of bitter storms.

Majestic man, enduring man of myriad visages,
continue to grow strong and tall
within the circle of my love.

From *Images of the African Diaspora*
in collaboration with artist Carl Owens

Sisters of the Sun

Cosmic African woman, mighty river
to whom all tributaries flow,
you are my pride and my delight.

From your varied faces emanates the splendor
of the rarest jewels of the universe — from the luminous
cool of pearl to the ruby's deepest radiance.

Daughters of a common land and sisters of the sun,
no matter where you flower, you are beautiful,
the ultimate creation of time and circumstance,

mysterious as an Egyptian cat, smooth
as a cowrie shell, colorful as a strip of kente cloth,
creative as braids of hair, ending and beginning

nowhere that can be defined. Cosmic African woman
of many faces, mighty river of my soul, my spirit flows
from you, returns forever to you
in an unbroken circle of love.

From *Images of the African Diaspora*
in collaboration with artist Carl Owens

II.

"I'm so glad trouble don't last always."
(Negro Spiritual)

Soon I Will Be Done

All my life I been waitin'
for trouble to pass.

If it wasn't a flood, it was a drought.
If it wasn't the boll weevil,
it was white folks tryin' to take our land.

Soon's we built a house big enough
for all the kids, they raised our taxes.

Then Papa died and Mama come to live with us
with all her furniture 'cause Brother say
we the onlies' ones with that much room.

Soon as Son got outa trouble
Suzie come up pregnant.

We was all so proud of Junior when he come back home
from Viet Nam with medals an' honors
an' his picture in the paper
till the polices gunned him down
robbin' a grocery store.
(Leas' that's what they told us.)

25

I use to sing in church
(an truly I did believe):
"Soon-a will be done with the troubles of the world,
Goin' home to live with God."

But I betcha anything,
soon's I get to heaven
the golden stairs is gonna fall down
and God's gonna say, "Sistuh Johnson,
see kin you give us a han' here."
Sure as anything, I'm gonna be the one
has to build 'em back up again.

The Old Women

They are young.
They do not understand
what the old women are saying.

They see the gnarled hands raised
and think they are praying.
They cannot see the weapons hung

between their fingers. When the mouths
gape and the rasping noises
crunch like dead leaves,

they laugh at the voices
they think are trying to sing.
They are young

and have not learned
the many faces of endurance, the furtive
triumphs earned through suffering.

Phillis*

I hardly remember my mother's face now
but I still feel
at my bosom a chill wind
stirring strange longings for the sturdy back
I used to lean against for warmth and comfort
when I had grown too tall to ride.

And I am blinded by
the glint of sunlight
striking golden fire from the flint
of seafoamed rocks below me
on some island not too far from home.

After that, the only light I saw
was a few wayward chinks of day
that somehow slanted into the airless tomb
where chains confined me motionless to a dank wall.

Then the sun died and time went out completely.
In that new putrid helltrap of the dead
and dying, the stench
of vomit, sweat, and feces

---

*Phillis Wheatley (1753-1784) was brought to this country from Senegal
West Africa, as a slave when she was about seven years old. She became a
poet representative of the best of the colonial period. Her rhymed couplets
were similar to those of Alexander Pope, whose work she admired.

28

mingled with the uneasy motion
of the ship until my senses failed me . . . . . .

I do not know how many weeks or months
I neither thought nor felt, but I awoke
one night — or day, perhaps —
revived by consciousness of sound.
I heard
the pounding of the waves against the shipside
and made believe its rhythm
was the speech of tribal drums
summoning in acute need the spirit
of my ancestors. I dreamed I saw
their carven images arrayed
in ceremonial austerity. I thought I heard
their voices thundering an answer
to my supplication: "Hold fast.
Sur / vive   sur / vive   sur / *vive!*"
And then I slept again . . . . . .

Once more the sunlight came, but not the same
as I remembered it. Now it sat silver-cold
upon the indifferent New England coast. Still
it was good to see the sun at all.
And it was something
to find myself the bright dark mascot
of a blind but well-intentioned host,
a toy, a curiosity, a child
taking delight in anyone's attention
after so long a death.

As I grew older, it was not enough.
That native lifesong once again burst free,
spilled over sands of my acquired rituals —
urged me to match the tribal rhythms
that had so long sustained me, that must
sustain me still. I learned to sing
A dual song:
> My fathers will forgive me if I lie
> For they instructed me to live, not die.
> "Grief cannot compensate for what is lost,"
> They told me. "Win, and never mind the cost.
> Show to the world the face the world would see;
> Be slave, be pet, conceal your Self — but be."

Lurking behind the docile Christian lamb,
unconquered lioness asserts: "I am!"

"The Sun Do Move"*

Who wouldn't believe,
who wouldn't,
who wouldn't believe?

Camp meeting outside
the city limits.
Corn-high, the yellow wave
of faith, gushing
on his word.

> And God said . . . .
> > *Preach it, brotha!*
> The Good Book reads . . . .
> > *Yes, it do, Lawd, it do!*

Day climbing over the southeast
corner of the earth,
grasping for the truth.
> *Tell it, John Jasper,*
> *Hallelujah!*

---

* John Jasper [1812-1893 or 1901], a former slave, believed the entire
Bible was literally true and, through exhaustive study, was able to "prove"
from Scripture the mobility of the sun and the flatness of the earth. His
famous sermon, "The Sun Do Move and the Earth Am Square," drew crowds
of worshipers to his church, as well as to all-day camp meetings in the
country. So thorough was his research, so convincing his sincerity and
powerful his oratory that even those who knew better were convinced, even
if only momentarily, of the authenticity of his claim.

31

All day long, all Sunday afternoon
the fields outside of Richmond rocking.
Sun melting down like lard
on the griddle of the world,
the hungry square of earth swallowing
it up again.
                    Come, Jesus!

Who wouldn't believe,
who wouldn't, who
wouldn't believe!

The Master Calls

(In appreciation of Rev. S.S. Jones)

Consider this: An Oklahoma black man in the 1920's
buys a movie camera, recognizing
that what transpires in his time and place
is worthy of remembrance.
Imagine him crossing the Atlantic on a steamship.

In the vestibule of Antioch Baptist Church,
1720 Emporia Street, Muskogee, a placard reads,
"The Master Calleth Me!" under his photograph.
Behind, a picture of a large stone structure with a cross.

Farewell Program!
Friday night, December 19th, 1924.
Dr. S.S. Jones,
The Business Pastor, Soul Winner,
Leader and Race-Builder.
Off for England, France, Switzerland, Italy,
Egypt, Abyssinia, and the Holy Land!
"God be with you."

On National Baptist Convention stationery
(S.S. Jones, D.D., corresponding secretary),
he writes my father: "Jerusalem, Palestine, 2/1/25.
My dear son, This is just to let you know
where your second father has gotten to.

33

I plan to visit you in New Jersey
as soon as possible after my return."

He gathers mustard seed from the Garden of Gethsemane,
picks up a broken stone from the Garden Tomb,
baptizes strangers in the Jordan River,
and from the bubbling crater of Mount Vesuvius
collects some souvenirs of lava.

The camera pans to East Orange and a Sunday
in 1926 after a summer rain. My mother,
slimmer and younger than I remember her,
chases my brother across the yard
trying to save him and his white suit from the puddle
he manages to slip in anyhow.
I am not allowed outside in the wet grass
for the picture-taking.
Mother, smiling with gold-edged teeth,
and Father, doffing his straw hat,
climb the steps to join me where I'm standing on a bench
at the back porch window, solemn-faced,
ribbon tied in a huge bow on my top braid.
They prompt me to wave a three-year-old *bye-bye.*

Back in Oklahoma, in an all-black town — Boley
or Grayson or Wybark — members of a family
file out of a sturdy brick house built with their own hands,
pose on the porch a moment, bow politely,
then turn and stiffly file back in.

People pick cotton and bale it on land that is theirs,
watch grasshoppers drill their own fields rich with oil.
A white aproned woman, hair pulled back in a bun,
scatters handfuls of feed to farmyard chickens.
Another, wearing a bonnet loosely tied under the chin,
hands her husband a large tin cup of water;
he pauses at a horse-drawn plow to drink.
A man in overalls pumps fuel at the Luther Gas Station.
While others wait their turn on the river bank,
a preacher clasps a woman's hands in one of his,
and with the other on her back, baptizes her.
She comes up from the water with her white robe clinging.
Uniformed Elks march and ride in cars and decorated wagons
in a grand parade, medals gleaming, trumpets raised.
A multitude follows a casket down an unpaved road.
Children holding hands stream out of school and spill
onto the playground, joyful in the sun.
Congregations emerge from churches, women
in high-collared dresses and wide-brimmed hats,
men removing theirs, as they approach the camera . . . .

The hours of viewing end. The all-black towns rewind,
people walking backward into time.

Tree of Heaven

(Ailanthus Altissima)

I will live.
The ax's angry edge against my trunk
cannot deny me. Though I thunder down
to lie prostrate among exalted grasses
that do not mourn me,
I will rise.

I will grow:
Persistent roots deep-burrowed in the earth
avenge my fall. Tentacles will shoot out swiftly
in all directions, stubborn leaves explode their force
into the sun.
I will thrive.

Curse of the orchard,
blemish on the land's fair countenance,
I have grown strong for strength denied, for struggle
in hostile woods. I keep alive by being the troublesome,
indestructible
stinkweed of truth.

Alabama Centennial

They said, "Wait." Well, I waited.
For a hundred years I waited
in cotton fields, kitchens, balconies,
in bread lines, at back doors, on chain gangs,
in stinking "colored" toilets
and crowded ghettos,
outside of schools and voting booths.
And some said, "Later."
And some said, "Never!"

Then a new wind blew, and a new voice
Rode its wings with quiet urgency,
Strong, determined, sure.

"No," it said. "Not 'never,' not 'later.'
Not even 'soon.'
Now.
Walk!"

And other voices echoed the freedom words.
"Walk together, children, don't get weary,"
Whispered them, sang them, prayed them, shouted them.
"Walk!"
And I walked the streets of Montgomery
Until a link in the chain of patient acquiescence broke.
Then again: Sit down!
And I sat down at the counters of Greensboro.

Ride! And I rode the bus for freedom.
Kneel! And I went down on my knees in prayer and faith.
March! And I'll march until the last chain falls
Singing, "We shall overcome."

Not all the dogs and hoses in Birmingham
Nor all the clubs and guns in Selma
Can turn this tide.
Not all the jails can hold these young black faces
From their destiny of manhood,
Of equality, of dignity,
Of the American Dream
A hundred years past due.
Now!

Midway

I've come this far to freedom and I won't turn back.
I'm climbing to the highway from my old dirt track.
        I'm coming and I'm going
        And I'm stretching and I'm growing
And I'll reap what I've been sowing or my skin's not black.

I've prayed and slaved and waited and I've sung my song.
You've bled me and you've starved me but I've still grown
                                strong.
        You've lashed me and you've treed me
        And you've everything but freed me
But in time you'll know you need me and it won't be long.

I've seen the daylight breaking high above the bough.
I've found my destination and I've made my vow,
        So whether you abhor me
        Or deride me or ignore me,
Mighty mountains loom before me and I won't stop now.

"Lord, I hear of show'rs of blessings . . .
Let some drops now fall on me."
— Elizabeth Cochner

Even Me

*(for Mildred Dobey and the Plymouth Renaissance Choir,
Detroit, Michigan)*

My Lord
wasn't no stuck-up man.
He was one of us.
He ran with common folks,
spoke up for street women
and lepers
and stuck by friends like Lazarus
when they had given up on life.
Smiled at black Simon
who shared his burden on
the road to Calvary.
And when they nailed him
to a cross,
he told one of the crooks
beside him
they could hang out together when they got
where they was goin'.

And even now
when I sometimes feel like
the bottom's dropped out
of everything,

he speaks to me and says,
"Come on, chil', you got somethin'
on your mind.
Let's you and me sit down awhile
an' talk about it."

My Jesus,
he ain't no stuck-up man.

Make Thy Way Plain

(for Professor Melva Wilson Costen,
Interdenominational Theological Center, Atlanta, Georgia)

Jesus, I'm standin' at the crossroads an' I don't know
which way to turn. You tol' me I was one of your children
an' you promised to take care of me one way or another,
no matter what, an' show me the way I'm suppose to go.
But sometimes I can't seem to hear you talkin' back to me
when I ask you for guidance. I want to do your will,
but nothin' I can think of makes any sense. I don't know
nobody else to get help from. My friends and loved ones
is so busy with their own problems they haven't got no time
to listen to mine. So I'm asking you, Jesus, from deep down
in my heart to tell me what I should do, which way
I should go. Lead me, Lord, please. Lay your way out plain
in front of me, 'cause I know you have the power to direct
an' keep me in all my ways. Amen.

Pilot Me

I don't sail no tempestuous seas, Lord,
but you know I have to deal with
these city streets and freeways every day
an' they is dangerous. What with

drive-by shootin's, drunk drivers
weavin' in an' out of traffic
and people talkin' on cell phones,
I don't feel like I got no control over anything.

You know I don't ask for much, Lord,
but I do wanna know that, when I
go off to work in the mornin' and try my best
to do the job the man is payin' me for

whether I feel like it or not, I can make it
back to my kids at night without gettin'
my brains blown out or somethin' else bad
happenin' to me along the way.

There sure is a lot of danger out there hidin'
around corners, but Jesus, they tell me

you are a "sovereign" and in charge
of everything, so please do steer me
in the right direction, watch over me,
protect me, and get me safely where I'm goin'.

"All I have needed Thy hand hath provided . . . ."
— Thomas O. Chisholm

Great is Thy Faithfulness

Lord, sometime I go to bed so weary and discouraged
I don' know how I can make it through the night, but
somehow
sleep come down on me like a whisper, an' in the mornin'
I wake up with the sun warm on my face all friendly like and
I get up singin'.

Other times my life be such a sizzle of anger and resentment
'cause somebody say somethin' 'bout me or do somethin'
mean
I almost burn to a crisp in the heat of my own rage
an' I be fussin' an' cussin' all over the place till I don' know
whether I'm comin' or goin'.

But then you send down your cool dew and settle it on my
spirit
jus' like that balm in Gilead they sing about in church and
suddenly
I feel all quiet an' calm inside. An' I say "Thank you, Jesus"
'cause you always seem to know exactly what to do
to make things right.

Seem like your friends don't always be there when you need
'em
but Lord, you never have failed me yet. You always been
there for me

45

unchangeable in all kind of weather an' in every season.
Whatever I need you always provide. You the only faithful
one, Jesus,
the only true an' faithful one.

"When the storms of life are raging, stand by me."

Stand by Me

*(in grateful memory of Charles A. Tindley, 1851-1933,
pioneer African American hymnist)*

My Jesus was a stand-by friend.
People in the Bible could always count on him
bein' there whenever they was down on their luck.

One time when he was sailin' with his buddies,
a sudden storm was fixin' to turn their boat over
and they all thought for sure they was gonna drown.
But he stood up calm as you please an' said, "Peace,
be still." An' them waters settled down jus' like lambs
an' the storm stopped ragin' and they was all able
to make it back to shore in one piece.

An' when Mary, the bad one, was fixin' to get stoned
to death for bein' a 'ho', he stepped in an' said:
"Hey, guys, how come you so sure what she's doin'
'less you been doin' it with her? If you don' wanna
deal with that, get lost." An' they all took off runnin'.
Then he tol' her, "Go on now an' don' do it no more."

My Lord was somethin' else, all right.
Still is, an' I can testify to that.
He's carried me through all my trials and tribulations
an' I've had more than my share of them.

Seem like I get tossed aroun' sometime just like a boat
in a storm. But I know I'm gonna make it through
'cause I got my stand-by friend walkin' with me, holdin'
my han', takin' up for me day after day after day.

"There is room enough in Paradise
in Glory."
(Negro Spiritual)

To Have a Home

Lord, I'm comin' to you 'cause I gotta talk to somebody
an' I know you understand. They musta tol' you,
the night you was born your mama and daddy was travelin'
an' couldn't find no place to spend the night.
Seem like all they could do was take the motel clerk up
on his offer to let 'em sleep out back in the barn with the
                    animals,
so the first thing you ever smelled in your life
wasn't no lilies of the field but cow dung.
An' even when you was a grown man you said
all the foxes and rabbits had homes they could go to
but you didn't have no place to lay your head.

So I know you know, Lord, how I feel
huddled up on this lumpy mattress
with my three kids curled up around each other
tryin' they best to keep warm. At least,
we out of the wind an' I'm thankful for that.
But I do wish we had a little place we could call our own,
some place where we could go to the toilet in peace
an' take a nice hot bath once in a while. I can't explain
to my babies how come we gotta keep on movin' like this
and never settlin' down nowhere.

49

Do we have to wait till we die an' get to heaven
to find room enough for my kids to spread out and grow in,
to have a real honest-to-goodness home?

"Take my hand, precious Lord, lead me home."

At the River I Stand

(In memory of Thomas A. Dorsey, 1900-1993)

Lord, it's gettin' late an' dark an' I'm gettin' tired.
I'm standin' here on the brink of chilly Jordan waitin'
for that ol' ship of Zion to carry me across. I feel
kinda hopeful 'cause I do wanna see you face to face
an' hear you tell me you know I did the best I could
under the circumstances. But to tell you the truth, Lord,
I'm feelin' kinda scared, too, 'cause I don' know
what it's gonna be like crossin' over. You always been
my light through every darkness and my salvation
in every storm, an' I could always count on you
to guide me through this vale of tears, showin' my feet
which way to go, holdin' my hand an' supportin' me
whenever I felt weak an' thought I was gonna fall.
So I'm really countin' on you now, sweet Jesus, now
with the shadows fallin' an' my fear of the night closin' in
                    on me
to stick even closer by me than usual. Keep on doin'
what you always been doin' only
maybe just a little bit more now, Lord,
just a little bit more.

51

III.

Attitude at 75

In this recurring dream I am Tina Turner
flinging my wild wig at the world,
strut-stomping across the stage
on miniskirted gams ageless and untamed,
completely in command and belting out my song,
"What's Time Got to Do with It!"

Letting It All Hang Out

Gray Strands

1. Badge of trial
    and triumph:
    It is mine, I have
    earned it.
    I wear it proudly.

2. There is nothing
    more lovely
    than silver framing
    a face
    of old ebony.

Girdle

1. Don't need this noose
    anymore.
    Won't choke myself with
    someone
    else's brand of rope.

2. Free now to ride
    the waves of
    the wind unbridled,
    to float
    on a crest of cloud.

Liberation

1. For the last time
   undo these
   thirteen fasteners
   of a
   longline, long-lie bra.

2. What if my once
   firm breasts sag?
   My fountain runs full
   and free.
   My children bless me.

Glories of the Morning

God's glorious goodmorning to the world
bursts forth in trumpets of translucent splendor
climbing on a vine of faith
and stretching to the sun.

My Mother's Roses

Meticulously she traced the pattern
on a pink silk panel,
oil-painted roses on green stems
of hope.
Some were buds and some
were full-blown possibilities.

It was the Thirties and times were grim,
but Mrs. Tilden's homegrown classes
in oil paints, beaded lampshades,
and crepe paper costumes for pageants
in the high school auditorium
beamed a ray of sunlight into dismal corners.

In our backyard there were no roses, only
a profusion of sunflowers and hollyhocks that flourished,
summer after summer, whether showers blessed them
or not, and lilies of the valley that multiplied
with no particular care.

But my mother's artificial roses, painted on silk dreams,
remind me still of gifts too long forgotten,
of sources of sustenance too long denied.

Beach Scene

(for "Tid" after fifty-three years)

We wiggle our toes in the white sands
of the beach at Pass-A-Grille,
our lives open to each other as the translucent
shells your grandchildren bring.

How roughly the winds have blown us,
how turbulently the waves of the Gulf surged
to scatter us so far apart, yet bring us back together
here in this special place of pain and peace.

Your daughter's spirit glides on the wings of seagulls,
hovers on the rim of the earth as the red sun lowers,
then slips beyond our view, leaving mauve streaks
across the deepening shadows of the sky.
> *I disappear for awhile but*
> *I will come again with the dawn.*
> *I will never leave you.*

We too rise in the daybreak of our renewal,
the abyss of years bridged with our latenight sharing.
Our spirits draw closer, strengthened by new insights
into who we were and who we have become.

This poem is a rare stone I found hidden in the sand.
Tuck it away in some secret place as a reminder
that we can sometimes find again what we have lost,
polished into new radiance, deeper splendor.

At Midday

(A birthday wish for Jill)

Woman to woman now, we tell our beads
on the worn rosary of years
together in the same slant of light.
No longer clay and potter,
we are what we have made each other,
your mark indelibly on me
as mine on you.

And so, at midday, I wish you
a taste of cururú and jaca fruit,
aroma of agogô bells at Carnival,
your fingers' touch on a berimbau,
and a silver balangandan hung with amulets.

May the *pretos velhos* endow you with their wisdom,
Yansan clear your path of storm and rain,
and Yemanjá protect and guide you
as you sail forever toward Brazilian shores.

CURURÚ: greens cooked with fish, pepper, and palm oil
AGOGÔ: double metal bell played at Carnival and condomblé rites
BERIMBAU: stringed instrument consisting of a bow, gourd and small
    stick
BALANGANDAN: a decorative piece of jewelry
PRETOS VELHOS: African ancestor spirits
YANSAN: Yoruba goddess of wind and storm
YEMANJÁ: goddess of the sea

Twice a Child

(for my mother at ninety)

Butterflies fan fragile, filmy wings
in the darkening forest I lead her through,
holding her hand, guiding her trembling
footsteps, buttoning her memory
as I used to dress my dolls
when she was mother
and I was child.
Now overhanging leaves
filter fading gold through shadow
to the damp and slippery ground beneath
as she drifts through the twilight
of a fairy tale whose characters' names
she has forgotten.
And I can only guess what distant bells she hears
tolling at the top of the hill
she climbs on all fours.

Reluctant Light

(in memory of Maude Selena Hilton Long)

Mother, I didn't mean to slight you but
it wasn't you that I adored.
You hid your energy in shadows
and I was dazzled by the sun.

I idolized the one whose voice soared to prophetic heights,
whose words rejuvenated epics of the ages. Some fine June
        Sundays,
slender and magnificent in morning coat, he would electrify
        the pulpit
with eloquent pronouncements of doom and glory so divine
the very gates of heaven seemed to part, bathing the
        atmosphere in crystal light.
Seeking his favor, I rehearsed raising my hand like his in
        benediction,
earning the childhood name of Preacher, shortened in time to
        Prete.

You gave us daily sustenance but there was never
a choir's fanfare or the soulbeat of the mighty to grant
        applause.
You baked the bread for which we seldom thanked you,
canned pears for winter and mended Depression-weary
        clothes,
scrubbing sheets on a washboard, humming hymns to lift
        your sagging spirit,

and cultivating beauty in endless flower pots.
The summer when he toured the streets of ancient Palestine
        and Rome,
you consoled yourself by painting pictures of the Appian
        Way
using the kitchen table for an easel.
You coached me with my homework, rejoiced
in my small triumphs and prepared me to confront the
        enemy,
tapping your umbrella against my fifth grade teacher's desk
to punctuate your firm demand for justice. I didn't recognize
your subtle power that led me through blind, airless caves,
your quiet elegance that taught me dignity — nor could I
        know
the wind that bore *him* high into the sunlight
emanated from your breath. I didn't want your journey,
rebelled against your sober ways.

But I have walked through my own shadows and, like you,
transcended glitter. I have learned
that I am source and substance of a different kind of light.

Now when they say I look like you and tell me
that I have deepened to your wisdom, softened
to your easy grace, I claim my place with honor
in that court of dusky queens whose strength and beauty
invented suns that others only borrow. And Mother,
I am glad to be your child.

Memorial

*(in memory of the reverend doctors Clarence M. Long,
Senior and Junior)*

Father, give them
a small room together
with water running fluid
as their thoughts
into a marble bowl
where they can probe
the electric air
with morning razors,
their lathered faces sharing
a mirror steamed up
with the sermons
they preach
to each other.

Lonely Eagle

(In memoriam: 1st Lt. Wilbur F. Long, 1920-1998)

My brother is up there somewhere
tunneling through a cloud,
once again a Redtail piloting his World War II P-51.

After his plane was shot down over Hungary
gashing his nose when he crashed-landed,
after the run from enemy pursuit, blood streaming down his
        face,

after Stalag Luft II in Germany and forced marches
to other prison camps, after liberation,
leaner, lice-infested, wearing the same clothes he was captured
        in,

after his safe return to family and home,
after piloting his cabin cruiser in Long Island Sound
(substitute for the plane he couldn't afford),

his wartime flight was what defined him all his years.
Driving alone through rush hour traffic now, I search the blue
to catch the shadow of the wings I know are there emerging.

Too far below to hear his engine, I feel his spirit
following me along the mundane freeway, I, earth-bound
and lonelier than the eagle he has become.

He Lives in Me

(in memory of Clarence Marcellus Long, Sr.)

My father was a strong and stalwart man.
Slight of build, he towered over cities
and had the might of armies.
Light of skin, he was the blackest man I knew.
In the unbeautiful years, he taught me pride;
when despair was ready to engulf me,
he rescued me with hope. By his hands,
in his arms, I was immersed in waters
of integrity and truth.
I learned my lessons at his knee:
> The just shall live by faith.
> If a beggar asks for food but isn't hungry,
>> that's his problem. If you turn him away
>> and he really is, it's yours
>> (and it isn't your responsibility
>> to take the measure of his guile
>> or honest need).
> If you see a toy with jagged edges
>> (any obstruction)
>> dropped on the floor or in the way,
>> it doesn't matter if you put it there
>> or not; you *see* it; you must remove it or
>> you're just as guilty (maybe more so)
>> as the one who left it there.

I am my father's daughter. I make no apologies
for being who I am, for having learned integrity
early in life — make no excuses that my neighborhood
was haven because my parents loved me
and loved each other
and made our home "rock in a weary land."
I go out of my way
to kick banana peels or broken glass
from sidewalks — try to remove obstacles, no matter
who put them there. I will not apologize.
I cannot speak of him in metaphor or symbol.
My father was upright, noble, and uncompromised,
and he gave me all I needed to be proud,
moral, and black — and whole. I can only praise him now
with hallelujahs, trumpets, cymbals, and drums.

Reply
(Wedding Song)

I cannot swear with any certainty
that I will always feel as I do now,
loving you with the same fierce ecstasy,
needing the same your lips upon my brow.
Nor can I promise stars forever bright
or vow green leaves will never turn to gold.
I cannot see beyond this present night
to say what promises the dawn may hold.
And yet, I know my heart must follow you
high up to hilltops, low through vales of tears,
through golden days and days of somber hue,
and love will only deepen with the years
becoming sun and shadow, wind and rain,
wine that grows mellow, bread that will sustain.

IV.

Souvenir

This is not what I meant to keep
I thought of bitter-bright rememberings
pressed petals of forget-me-nots
or once-bold daffodils

not
this hardness,
not
these brittle stalks of
weeds

Nocturne II: Still

Midnight streetlights beckon me
to a certain house on a certain nameless street.
The windows are darkly shuttered.
Somewhere behind them (having yawned
through newsmen's dooms an hour ago) you sleep.
I ease my car into the blueblack peace,
the fretful motor purring, purring now.

Were you to stir and glance into the throbbing night,
you would see only a long still shadow
across an ordinary street.
You would not sense the heavy-blossomed fuschia
                    branches —
you would forget that it is April once again.

Blow out the candle as you will.
The farthest star still watches, the loneliest shadow
leans toward you still.

Trinity: A Dream Sequence, #18

Stark day corrodes the silver of the dream
a little, yes.
And caution insulates gloved fingers now
against enchantment of a certain touch.
But the splendor does not vanish
because you avert your eyes
nor the music cease to quiver
because your words are quick and cold.

I had to tell you.
Turn away if you must; I always knew
that you would have to turn away.

Still I can sing you songs
in silences more eloquent
than hope or triumph.

Severance

If you have forgotten, then I say
I have forgotten, too.
I give you back your soul
and send you gladly on your way.

Whenever a new moon rises,
an old sun sets. I know that,
and I know I have to let you go.

But when dreams, wild as prairie broncos,
burst from their bonds
and gallop toward each other
defying choice and wisdom,
sleep has no tether that can keep them apart.

Without Condition

All these years
I have loved you
without condition of return,

laid my sacrifices
at the altar
of your need.
Spring

never spiraled through
reluctant soil without
my touch, or
summer

surged through sun
and azure wind
without my presence
at your rebirth.

I have wished you
cardinals and lemonade,
lake water stroking your hand,
sunrise

and songs
my frail voice could not
sing but only
say.

When the first
green leaf turned
scarlet or gold,
I have been

there always.
When winter blanketed
dead leaves in snow, I have
been there.

So what if now
another voice sustains you,
another hand teaches you what
love means?

It's all right, it really is
all right because

I have loved you all
these years
without
condition of return.

Packrat

My trouble is
I always try to save
everything

old clocks and calendars
expired words buried
in open graves

But hoarded grains of sand
keep shifting as rivers
redefine boundaries and seasons

Lengths of old string
rolled into neat balls
neither measure nor bind
nor do shelves laden with rancid sweets
preserve
what ants continually nibble away

Love should be eaten
while it is ripe
and then the pits discarded

Lord give me at last
one cracked bowl holding
absolutely nothing

Sylvester Expelled

"Mene, mene, tekel, upharsin."
(Thou art weighed and found wanting.)

Predictable, the easy lie
that swings back like a boomerang,
the swaggering gait, the darting eye
that turns aside the reprimand,
seeking in vain to nullify
the guilty trap of circumstance.

The pattern fits; the type is known;
the punishment is swift and sure.
Familiar is the stormy frown
that now confronts the one-way door.
The verdict: *Out.* Direction: *Down.*
We lean back justified, secure.

But he knows what we cannot guess
and reads time better than we taught.
Potential for the infamous
is higher than the grades he got.
The cryptic message is for us
who never learned what *we* are not.

Images

1.

One student (white),
leading a class discussion
of *Native Son*
and running out of things to say,
asked, "How would you feel
if you encountered Bigger Thomas
on a dark street
late at night?"

Another student (black, astute)
countered: "How
would you know it was
Bigger Thomas?"

2.

I pictured him as muscular,
dull-eyed and dense, his sullen scowl,
skin color, maze of hair
and criminal demeanor defining
my most horrendous nightmare.

How can I reconcile
that image
with this tender yellow
boy who could have been
my son?

And When

and when the door creaked open again
and he pulled back the covers and soothed
it's okay, baby, daddy just wants to show
his little girl how much he loves her

and even though she pleaded and her strangled tears
soaked in the pillow and he kept on plunging
and when three months passed and the flow
didn't come even though she prayed and

Jesus' redemptive blood refused to save her
from her ballooning belly and when
his quick eyes warned *don't tell* and she wondered
if the child would make her mother or sister

and when she leapt from the bridge
knowing she would surely go to hell,
still she had no answer to the question
Whose guilt? Whose intended murder?

A Thousand Goodbyes

"Last year, the shelter took in almost 24,000 dogs, cats and other animals. Less than a third were adopted or reclaimed by owners. The rest found their way to [the retiring employee who] killed more than 13,000 of them, one at a time, with injections of sodium pentabarbitol .... 'You have to understand that you are doing the best thing,' she said."

("Animals' friend bids a thousand good-byes,"
Detroit Free Press, June 23, 1989)

1.

If they would let her near them,
she would put them in a carrier
and take them to be spayed and neutered,
but they are wild. They belong to no one
but have found shelter in her garage.
Litter after litter, they give birth
in loft or barrel. She finds their footprints
on her windshield.

2.

Headlights in her driveway pick up the gleam
of feline eyes. The kittens crouch in tall wet grasses
and day lilies bent by rain. The cat lady calls
in highpitched invitation to the feast she sets
for them in paper plates. When she goes inside
young and old scamper to the side door.
In time they will grow bolder but never tame.

3.

They tumble over each other, pouncing and biting
each other's tails, leaping to catch a fly
or chase an errant leaf across the driveway.
The cat lady watches from her window.

4.

Roaming dogs have killed another kitten.
In the morning its carcass glares open-eyed
at the angry sky. The mother cat sniffs the still form.
Her wail is the grief of ages. Even after the remains
have been deposited in decent plastic and removed,
she crouches near the spot and cries all day
and will not come when the cat lady calls.

5.

The cat lady keeps on calling. Generation after generation,
they come. They are born, they give delight
a little while before they are destroyed,
and the anguish clouding the air makes her question why
a sparrow's fall is more significant.

The Last Happy Day

(for Alfred and Irene Williams, in memoriam)

July Photographs

1. The Godchild and Her Daughter

The prepubescent girl circles her mother's waist
with spindly arms growing too fast for her body.
Behind them a jovial sun dazzles the depths of green
and scarlet in leaves and blood-ripe roses.

Just out of sight, the old pair
whose love is deep-rooted as ancient olive trees
smile at their little girl
now grown to womanhood and mother of the child.

Nobody asks, "Where will tomorrow take us?" Enough
to be together here encircled by a wreath of sunlit love.

> *We too have grown gnarled together.*
> *We count the common rings*
> *in the trees we have become.*
> *Our roots sink into deep soil*
> *and our bark is impervious*
> *to wind and weather.*

2. The Man

Cameras catch the sunlight's vigor
dancing in his eyes. In the velvet dark
his face turns like a sunflower to the brightness
he can no longer see. His fingers remember
the soil's rich balm, the profusion of petals —
daylilies and roses — splashed with gold.
His laughter is a deep-throated bird among them.

Suddenly a shadow falls
across his brow, his hair's
cool silver the one
remaining light.

> *Nine days to doom*
> *nine days to paradise.*
> *One perfect hour before*
> *the daylight dies.*

Sequel: The Woman

Summer does not dissolve
to autumn, then winter
but jolts and quakes
as the widow's tears
gush in vain to soothe and mend
the broken earth.

December Finale

1. And then,
as though his spirit called her
(but not so full of terror
and surprise!)
as though
he spoke her name
(but never wishing her goodness
to deliver her to evil!)
she was wrenched away.

2. Morning and conversation with a friend,
interrupted by insistent jangling at the door.
"The boy is back, says he dropped the lunch
I packed for him. Claims somebody in a car
was chasing him. I'd better hang up now.
Talk to you later."

                    Stealthy fingers rifle
the open purse. How to confront him, how
reprimand the audacity of one so frequently
befriended? Suddenly, raw energy unleashed,
animal eyes ferocious. Phone yanked from mooring
by hands no longer boy's but brutal hammers pounding,
bashing. A single scream for him who can
no longer hear, whose blind eyes, even if he could
be with her, would leave him helpless to defend.
Then the length of rope produced from nowhere,

whipped into place, stretched taut against tender
flesh, vulnerable cartilage. The mouth open
gasping for air, the bulging eyes pleading until
the kindness of eternal dark engulfs her.

> *By what shall we remember you? Not*
> *the eggs spilled on the kitchen floor*
> *or the now rotting meat intended to relieve*
> *his savage hunger. Not your stifled wail*
> *beating forever against our throats, or the sound*
> *of your head bumping down the basement steps —*
> *the congealed blood under the pulp of your face —*
> *the broomstick left protruding from your anus.*

> *Ironic now the photographs in summer's*
> *idyllic garden on the last happy day*
> *we shared. But "nothing worth keeping*
> *is ever lost in this world." Even in this world*
> *may the love-deep roots of trees*
> *conquer evil's senseless blight*
> *and the perennial flowering of your memory*
> *sustain us through whatever winter weather*
> *we still may know.*

Refuge

The endless fog winds
down a gray eternity
as quiet as death.

Shaggy brows brooding,
a deserted house keeps watch
with its blinded eyes.

Hide me, leaves of trees,
roofs of houses; oh, hide me,
secret veils of night.

Fear-removed to shores
not of my seeking, I find
harbors that are home.

Mortality

This is the surest death
of all the deaths I know.
The one that halts the breath,
the one that falls with snow
are nothing but a peace
before the second zone
for Aprils never cease
to resurrect their own,
and in my very veins
flows blood as old as Eve.
The smallest cell contains
its privileged reprieve.
But vultures recognize
this single mortal thing
and watch with hungry eyes
when Hope starts staggering.

City Nights

(for Gertrude and Eddie)

My windows and doors are barred
against the intrusion of thieves.
The neighbors' dogs howl in pain
at the screech of sirens.
There is nothing you can tell me
about the city
I do not know.

On the front porch it is cool and quiet
after the high-pitched panic passes.
The windows across the street gleam
in the dark.
There is a faint suggestion of moon-shadow
above the golden street light.
The grandchildren are asleep upstairs
and we are happy for their presence.

The conversation comes around to Grampa Henry
thrown into the Detroit River by an Indian woman
seeking to save him from the sinking ship.
(Or was he the one who was the African prince
employed to oversee the chained slave-cargo,
preventing their rebellion, and for reward
set free?)
The family will never settle it; somebody lost
the history they had so carefully preserved.

Insurance rates are soaring.
It is not safe to walk the streets at night.
The news reports keep telling us the things
they need to say: The case
is hopeless.

But the front porch is cool and quiet.
The neighbors are dark and warm.
The grandchildren are upstairs dreaming
and we are happy for their presence.

Renewal

June is forever and forever returning.
Howling headlines will not prevent it.
Statistics cannot deny that which will be.

In my springtime heart I know that earth
will have its way. October, that old faker,
coloring its leaves in deceptive gaiety,

all the time meaning brittleness and brown
death, doesn't fool me. December's
snowflakes and gossamer enticements, hiding

sludge and dirt under the wings of Christmas
angels, can't forever deceive. I know
what I know. There is something in the nature

of things that is assuring, that tells me the people
emerging from their dark lives to front porches
and sunlight when the warm days come

know the secret the universe sometimes tries
to conceal. Life forever rejuvenates
itself. Whatever else happens, life lives.

About the Author

Naomi Long Madgett has been Poet Laureate of the City of Detroit since 2001. Her first small collection of poems was published in 1941 when she was seventeen years old. Since then her work has appeared in numerous magazines and journals and more than 180 anthologies in this country and abroad.

Among her many honors are an American Book Award, the Michigan Artist Award, induction into three halls of fame, three honorary degrees including a Doctor of Fine Arts from Michigan State University, and an Alain Locke Award. The documentary film, *A Poet's Voice* (Vander Films), based on her award winning *Octavia and Other Poems* (Third World Press), won a Gold Apple Award of Excellence from the National Educational Media Network. *Pilgrim Journey: A Memoir* is forthcoming.

The Naomi Long Madgett/Lotus Press Archive was purchased last year by the Special Collections Library at The University of Michigan in Ann Arbor. (Some earlier papers are available in the Special Collections Library at Fisk University.)

Madgett has been publisher and editor of Lotus Press, Inc. since 1972 and has launched numerous poets on their careers. The annual Naomi Long Madgett Poetry Award, sponsored by Lotus Press, provides African American poets in particular an opportunity for recognition and publication.

The author is professor of English emeritus at Eastern Michigan University.